Your Life as a SETTLER in Colonial America

by Thomas Kingsley Troupe
illustrated by C.B. Canga

PICTURE WINDOW BOOKS
a capstone imprint

Thanks to our advisers for their expertise, research, and advice:

Kevin Byrne, PhD, Professor of History
Gustavus Adolphus College, Saint Peter, Minnesota

Terry Flaherty, PhD, Professor of English
Minnesota State University, Mankato

Editor: Jill Kalz
Designer: Ashlee Suker
Art Director: Nathan Gassman
Production Specialist: Danielle Ceminsky
The illustrations in this book were created digitally.

Picture Window Books
1710 Roe Crest Drive
North Mankato, MN 56003
www.capstonepub.com

Library of Congress Cataloging-in-Publication Data
Troupe, Thomas Kingsley.
  Your life as a settler in Colonial America / by Thomas Kingsley Troupe
; illustrated by C.B. Canga.
       p. cm. — (The way it was)
  Includes index.
  ISBN 978-1-4048-7156-4 (library binding)
  ISBN 978-1-4048-7251-6 (paperback)
  1. United States—Social life and customs—To 1775—Juvenile
literature. 2. Colonists—United States—Social life and customs—17th
century—Juvenile literature. 3. Colonists—United States—Social life
and customs—18th century—Juvenile literature. I. Canga, C. B., ill.
II. Title.
  E162.T76 2012
  973.2—dc23   2011029598

Photo Credits:
Shutterstock: Kenneth V. Pilon, 3 (map), 31 (map)

Printed in the United States   5657

Your Role

Congratulations! You'll be playing the role of Colin Smalley in our play "Life in Colonial America." It's April 1762. You're an 11-year-old boy who lives with his family in the town of Williamsburg, Virginia.

You'll sleep on a hay-filled sack and go to the bathroom in an outhouse. You'll be up for chores before sunrise. Oh, and there's lots of homework. But you'll learn a valuable trade and make your father proud.

Tough life! **You ready?**

ACTION!

Duty Calls

Here in bustling Williamsburg, everyone has a job to do. There are shopkeepers and blacksmiths, shoemakers and tailors. Some people lay bricks. Others make wigs. Even a boy like you has a job. Your job right now? Go to school!

"Hurry, Colin!" your sister Mary shouts. "You're going to be late!" She runs off to a small white house. You run to a schoolhouse just down the road.

Young boys and girls in Colonial America
often learned letters, numbers, and some
reading in a dame school. These schools were held
in a teacher's home. After graduating from dame
school, boys went on to elementary school.
Most girls, however, were kept at home. There
they learned to sew, knit, and cook.

Listen and Learn

You slide into your seat with your hornbook and Bible. An older boy is already reading aloud. You carefully open your jar of ink and dip your quill pen into it. Yesterday your classmate Henry spilled his ink. He was lashed across the knuckles for being clumsy. You open your Bible and begin copying a passage. Tomorrow Mr. Brown, your teacher, wants you to recite the words.

Not too bad now, but during winter this room gets cold! Each student had to bring a piece of wood to school each day for the building's stove. Anyone who forgot was punished and made to sit in the coldest part of the room. Brrr!

Hornbooks were made of wood and shaped like paddles. Lesson sheets were attached to one side. They included the alphabet, vowel-consonant combinations, and prayers. A hornbook often had a hole drilled through the handle. It could then be tied to a child's belt or strung around his or her neck.

Little Time for Games

School lets out at noon, and you are supposed to hurry home to eat. But your friend George asks you to play a game of bowling. "Just one toss," you say. George hands you the ball. You aim for the wooden pins and roll it hard. The ball wobbles down the dusty path and knocks all but one pin down. "Maybe just one more," you say, setting up the pins again.

Children in Colonial America enjoyed all
sorts of activities. Marbles, board games,
and cricket were popular. So was quoits.
In that game, children tried tossing
a ring onto a stake.

Midday Meal

When you finally get home, your sister Elizabeth has just finished spooning out the stew.

"Look who decided to join us," your father says. His face and hands are black from working in the blacksmith shop. You apologize, say a prayer, and dig in. You dip stale bread into your bowl and wash it down with warm milk. You've eaten venison stew with corn and potatoes all week. But it's still tasty.

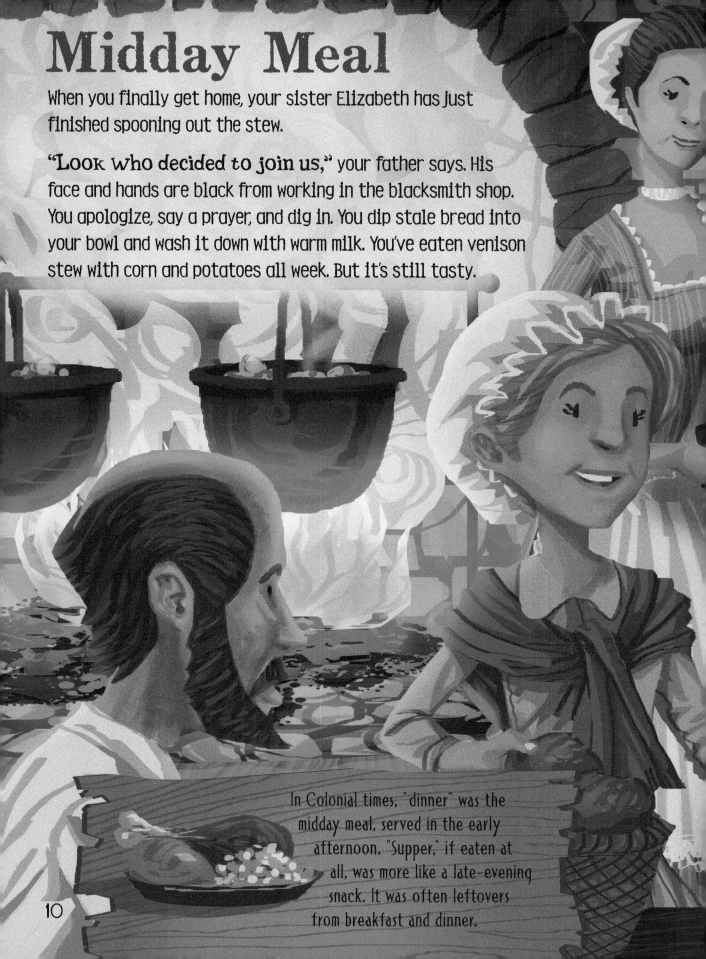

In Colonial times, "dinner" was the midday meal, served in the early afternoon. "Supper," if eaten at all, was more like a late-evening snack. It was often leftovers from breakfast and dinner.

Be extra nice to your mom and older sister, Colin. They've been getting dinner ready for hours. In Colonial America, it was the women's job to **pick** the vegetables, **bake** the bread, and **cook** the meals. Everything, at every meal, was homemade. **No fast food here!**

Not So Keen on Hygiene

You help your father all afternoon. Later, after a quick supper, he says, "We have a lot more work tonight, Colin. If you need to use the necessary, do it now." You quickly head to the outhouse. When you're finished, you throw a small shovelful of dirt into the hole.

On your way back, you find your sisters washing up. They wipe their faces and hands with a wet cloth. Everyone's hair and clothes are dirty, but a quick wipe once a day is good enough.

Toothbrushes were a luxury in Colonial America. Few people had them. Without brushing, teeth often rotted. They either fell out or were pulled.

Young Apprentice

Your real education comes from your father. You work with him in the blacksmith shop in the afternoons and evenings. "Mr. Carver's carriage wheel needs new rims," he says. He slips an iron bar into the forge.

You watch as the metal slowly turns bright orange, then yellow. With a pair of tongs, you pull it out and place it on the anvil. Your father hands you a hammer. You begin to bang the iron into shape. Sparks fly.

Blacksmiths in Colonial America made a number of things from metal. In addition to wheel rims, they made pots and pans, farming tools, and fireplace racks. They even made gates, chains, and locks.

Hit the Hay

It's late when you and your father lock up the blacksmith shop. You practice reciting your Bible passage on the walk home.

In the house your sisters and mother are pulling out the beds. The mattresses are old sacks, stuffed with rags, hay, and other soft things. You all say your prayers, and the light is put out.

Many homes during Colonial times didn't have separate bedrooms. To save space, some people built beds that folded into the wall.

Get Dressed

Good morning! What are you going to wear today? Same thing you wear every day! Like most of your fellow colonists, you own only a few pieces of clothing.

hat: three-cornered

shirt: longer, almost to the knees; also used as a sleeping gown

coat: unlined

breeches: pants that went to the knees

stockings: socks pulled up to the knees

garters: straps to hold stockings in place

shoes: dark-brown leather

silk gown: a dress-like covering for the gown petticoat with ruffled sleeves

shift: a long dress-like shirt; also used as a sleeping gown

stomacher: a piece of fabric pinned to the front of a gown to cover a stay

pocket: a pouch-like bag tied around the waist

stay: a piece of fabric with boning inside that laces up the back, like a girdle

apron: a long piece of fabric worn over the front of a gown

gown petticoat: a full skirt worn over hoops

hoops: a series of circles worn around the waist to keep a dress's shape

shoes: leather with buckles

Very young boys in Colonial America wore dress-like frocks. When they grew older (between 3 and 7 years old), they moved from skirts to pants. This change was called "breeching." The colonists thought of breeching as the start of a boy becoming a little man.

Chores Galore

The sun isn't fully awake yet, but you and the chickens are. You toss them some dried corn, collect eggs, and clean the coop. Next you milk the cow.

The rest of the family is busy too. Elizabeth is out fetching water. Mary is at the spinning wheel. Father is at the loom. Mother hands you a bowl of steaming porridge. **"Eat this and then you and Mary run off to school,"** she says. She then heads outside to start gathering today's vegetables.

Hard work was an important value in Colonial America. Boys and girls as young as 3 years old learned to pitch in and help.

Carver's Carriage

The streets buzz with activity. Through the noise someone shouts, "Colin! Colin Smalley!" You look and see Mr. Carver in his carriage. "Hello, Mr. Carver," you say. "I helped Father fix your wheel yesterday." Mr. Carver tips his hat. "And a fine job you did, lad," he says. "Hop in! I'll take you two to school."

You and Mary climb in. The inside is fancy. A patterned cloth covers the walls and seats. Mary leans over and whispers, "I feel like a princess!"

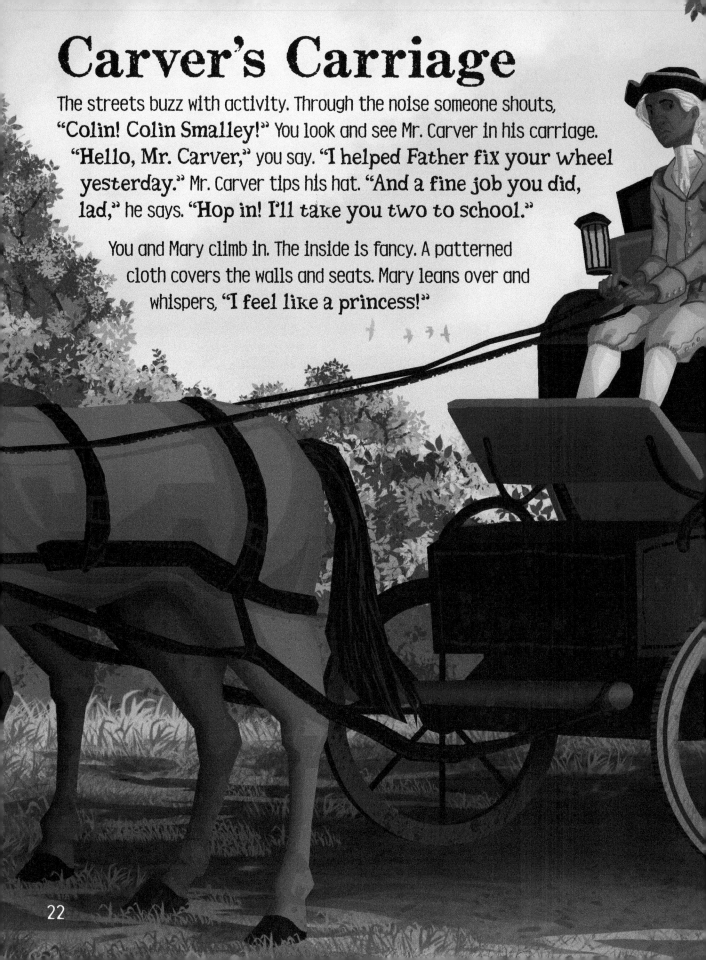

Now this is the way to travel, huh, Colin? Transportation in Colonial America wasn't easy. Few folks could afford a horse, let alone a carriage. Most people **walked** wherever they needed to go. But since they grew much of their own food and worked at home, **they didn't need to go far!**

Slavery

You pass the church, the silversmith, and a number of taverns. Slave women bustle in and out of the marketplace. They carry baskets of fresh meat and vegetables, cloth, and other household items. Your family doesn't have enough money to own slaves. But many others do. Men in your father's shop often gossip about runaway slaves and beatings. Your father tries to quiet them when you're around, but you still hear plenty.

In 1762, roughly half the population of Williamsburg was African American. Most, but not all, were slaves. Their duties included cooking, washing, tending horses, and gardening. They worked seven days a week and often lived in lofts above kitchens or stables.

Young Love

"There's James, bothering Elizabeth again," Mary says, rolling her eyes. You smile. "She'll likely marry him one day," you say. "And then they'll start a family of their own, in their own house." Mary wrinkles her nose at the idea and runs to school.

In the 1800s, boys and girls in their late teens would court one another with the idea of marrying one day. In the South, the wedding was often held in the groom's family's house. The party afterward was usually held at the bride's family's home.

Head of the Class

As soon as the bell rings, Mr. Brown asks you to recite your verses. You're nervous. You think about Roger. He had to wear a cone-shaped hat all day for forgetting his lessons. George laughed at him and got two smacks across his backside with a switch. You close your eyes and breathe. And before you know it, you're done. No mistakes. The class claps, and Mr. Brown nods.

I'm so glad you studied last night, kid. During Colonial times, students who didn't learn quickly enough often had to wear signs around their necks that said "FOOL." Teachers were **very strict** with their students back then.

A Star Is Born!

Will you listen to that crowd? **They loved you!** It was hard work living in Colonial America, but you did it. And guess what? Tomorrow you can sleep late (no chicken coop to clean) and use an indoor toilet!

Glossary

apprentice—someone who learns a trade by working with a skilled person

forge—a furnace in which metal is heated so it can be hammered into shape

hygiene—things that must be done to keep people and their surroundings clean

loom—a machine people use to make cloth

recite—to repeat something from memory

tavern—a place where people can buy and drink alcoholic beverages

venison—the meat of a deer

Index

African Americans, 24, 25
chores, 3, 20, 21, 30
clothing, 12, 18–19
cooking, 5, 10, 11, 25
family, extended, 17
food, 10, 11, 20, 23, 24
games, 8, 9
jobs, 3, 4, 11, 14, 15, 16
marriage, 27
outhouses, 3, 12

prayers, 7, 10, 16
punishment, 6, 24, 28, 29
school, 3, 4, 5, 6, 7, 8, 22, 27, 28, 29
slavery, 24, 25
sleeping, 3, 16, 18, 19, 30
teeth, 12
transportation, 22, 23
washing, 12, 25

More Books to Read

Sherman, Patrice. *How'd They Do That in Colonial America*. How'd They Do That? Hockessin, Del.: Mitchell Lane Publishers, 2010.

Studelska, Jana Voelke. *Women of Colonial America*. We the People. Minneapolis: Compass Point Books, 2007.

Winters, Kay. *Colonial Voices: Hear Them Speak*. New York: Dutton Children's Books, 2008.

Internet Sites

FactHound offers a safe, fun way to find Internet sites related to this book. All of the sites on FactHound have been researched by our staff.

Here's all you do:

Visit *www.facthound.com*

Type in this code: 9781404871564

 Check out projects, games and lots more at **www.capstonekids.com**

Look for All the Books in the Series: